Ax or Ask?

THE AFRICAN AMERICAN GUIDE TO BETTER ENGLISH

GARRARD McCLENDON, Ph.D.

Duthga Press - Chicago

Duthga Press LLC
McClendonReport.com
PO Box 81052
Chicago, IL 60681
800-975-6044

Copyright © 2018 Garrard McClendon, Ph.D.

All rights reserved. No part of this book may be reproduced or copied in physical or electronic form without permission from the publisher.

ISBN-13: 978-0996883214

Library of Congress Control Number: 2017911787

McClendon, Garrard O., 1966 -
Ax or Ask?: The African American Guide to Better English.

ISBN 978-0996883214 (paperback).
1. English Language - Rhetoric
2. English Language Style.
3. Black History.
4. African Americans
5. Linguistics.
6. Test Scores.
7. Black Speech Patterns.
8. Ebonics.
9. Black English.
10. Racism
11. Education.
12. Schools

Printed in the United States of America

DEDICATION

To my parents for the gift of life and an amazing education

To my wife for love and support during my challenges

To my brothers for clearing the path

CONTENTS

Children Left Behind	1
A Time and a Place for Black English	9
My Ebonics Story	19
Forbidden Words, Phrases, Definitions, & Pronunciations	23
The Origin of Black English Dialect	69
Black Leaders Use Mainstream English	77
Good and Evil in the Language of Hip Hop	81
Teach Mainstream English to Black Children	85
Expert Commentary on Black English	91
References	95

CHILDREN LEFT BEHIND

At an alarming rate, Black children are left behind in school. The sad reality is that very few decision-makers seem to care about children with poor standardized test scores. Children suffering from functional illiteracy are considered to be unmotivated delinquents with deviant cultural influences and low expectations.

Parents should seriously inquire about their children's teachers. Where were the educated? What are their teaching methods? Will they correct my child's English? Subsequently, teachers need to be thorough in knowledge as well as emotionally connecting to their students. Black children are left behind because of excuses, exoneration, and exhaustion in the classroom. Making excuses for children does not lead to progress; instead, it encourages inadequate progress. Students who are exonerated suffer from social promotion, which can lead to an illiterate 12th grader. Teacher exhaustion and burn-out can create a volatile school environment leading to a chaotic lack of discipline. When discipline disappears, learning may cease. And so is the case with undisciplined classroom teachers that allow Black children to speak as they wish in the classroom, with no correction of English. Teachers who are afraid to correct a child's speech do that child an enormous disservice, which will lead to ridicule and poor language arts skills in future learning environments.

Schools tend to ignore the ever-present mindset of anti-intellectualism pervading in the Black community. Christopher Jencks and Meredith Phillips (The Black-White Test Score Gap) found that on standardized tests, Black students perform 25% lower than Whites and Asians, and that this gap appears before kindergarten and continues into adulthood. There are no studies that prove that Blacks are genetically inferior, contrary to Herrnstein and Murray's *The Bell Curve: Intelligence and Class Structure in American Life*. But if Black children are taught from birth that everything related to education is negative, we've already failed them before their first day of school.

Leaving a child behind isn't difficult. American public schools, parents, teachers, and administrators do this daily by encouraging an anti-intellectual environment. Schools that ignore etiquette will invite rude and disrespectful behavior. Schools that do not encourage a strong moral fiber will suffer from weak leadership and a fractured value system. Academic environments that do not correct counter productive behavior will eventually suffer from irreversible apathy and entropy. And schools that do not teach standard mainstream English proficiency will produce students who will become victims of social promotion, passed from kindergarten through 12th grade without being able to write a complete sentence.

Generally, a child that does poorly in school doesn't have support from guardians at home. A lack of books in the home, limited cultural event participation (museums, theater, music, art), and a discouraging environment can also lead to apathy. Self-fulfilling prophecy can limit potential as well and it is a teacher's responsibility to give the child a sense of accomplishment and self-esteem.

Claude Steele's studies at Stanford University found that "stereotype threat" is quantifiable. This phenomenon states: if a student feels he is part of a group that has been negatively stereotyped, the student is likely to perform poorly if he thinks people might evaluate him through that stereotype.

Are standardized tests biased? Yes, but parents, teachers, and administrators must emphasize that most standardized tests have a math and verbal vantage point. In an article appearing in Capitalism Magazine, Walter Williams highlights comments by John McWhorter, author of *Losing the Race: Self Sabotage in the Black Community.*
McWhorter states that Blacks embrace anti-intellectualism, victimology, and separatism. He goes on to say that "so-called
politicians and so-called civil rights leaders have sold the commodity of victimhood to Black youngsters, teaching them that racism is invincible and that no individual effort can destroy it."

Booker T. Washington once said that, "...there is a class of colored people who make a business of keeping troubles, wrongs, and hardships of the Negro race [in front of the public]. Some people do not want the Negro to lose his grievances, because they do not want to lose their jobs."

McWhorter says that Blacks view educational achievement as *for Whites only*, therefore creating a Black

Cult of Anti-Intellectualism, which deems scholarly achievement as treachery.

Low expectations can damage a child's mental image of achievement. According to a study conducted in the state of California, Asian American parents view a low grade as an A- or B+, while White parents view a low grade as a C, and Black parents view a low grade as a D+.

Akilah Rogers, an Evanston Township High School student stated that getting good grades is connected to being White. Many Black students perpetuate the discouragement of education by teasing fellow Black students who strive for academic achievement. "Are you going to be White and achieve? Are you going to be Black and fail?" It is time to demonstrate to African American children that being intelligent is their right, and not just a privilege.

In a journal article called "Teacher Expectations Matter" by Nicholas Papageorge, Seth Gershenson, Kyungmin Kang, white teachers expect less academic success from black students than black teachers do from the same students. The researchers found that "white and other non-black teachers were 12 percentage points more likely than black teachers to predict black students wouldn't finish high school." Here are findings from the John Hopkins study.

- Non-black teachers were 5 percent more likely to predict their black boy students wouldn't graduate high school than their black girls.
- Black female teachers are significantly more optimistic about the ability of black boys to complete high school than teachers of any other demographic group. They were 20 percent less likely than white teachers to predict their student wouldn't graduate high school, and 30 percent less likely to say that then black male teachers.
- White male teachers are 10 to 20 percent more likely to have low expectations for black female students.
- Math teachers were significantly more likely to have low expectations for female students.
- For black students, particularly black boys, having a non-black teacher in a 10th grade subject made them much less likely to pursue that subject by enrolling in similar classes. This suggests biased

expectations by teachers have long-term effects on student outcomes.

A TIME AND A PLACE FOR BLACK ENGLISH

Good English, well spoken and well written will open more doors than a college degree. Bad English will slam doors you didn't even know existed.

William Raspberry

Discrimination has many disguises, but in America these forms are becoming more covert. A person's height, weight, gender, ethnicity, family name, bank account, and zip code can all be sources for discriminating against an individual. Faulty vernacular, vocabulary, articulation, enunciation, and diction can also be used to exclude certain citizens from opportunities and occupations. Black people must improve their speaking skills to avoid the pitfalls of exploitation, exclusion, and economic illiteracy.

Knowing the language of power and finance is gaining clout, not selling out.

Wearing jeans and sandals to an interview for a bank position would be self-sabotage. Though this may sound like a ridiculous example, you would be surprised how many people dress inappropriately for such important meetings. Similar to this practice stands the case of how language is inadvertently and inappropriately used in formal situations. Unfamiliar slang, Black Vernacular English, and foul language can hinder a candidate's chances of getting a job -- or keeping one. Loose language may also decrease the interviewer's interest or respect. A candidate must try her best in adhering to the rules of Standard American English, because being understood is the hallmark of communication.

If eight out of ten candidates are eliminated in the application process, it's a strong possibility that the eight eliminated didn't have the qualifications. There's also a chance they turned in subpar applications and dossiers. Many people don't proofread their applications and some mistakes can be as simple as misspelling your name. If you are one of the two chosen to have an interview, you must now pass stage two. The purpose of the interview will be to find a candidate who will be the most productive and who will best represent the company. Your interviewing skills must be flawless. Your clothes, hairstyle, accessories, cologne, facial expression, knowledge of the company, and diction must all be on-point. Subconsciously, the employer is eliminating candidates instantly and this is due to first impressions. In the book *More Power To You* by Glaser and Smalley, the authors discuss what sociologists call the "halo effect." This means that if you're viewed positively within the critical first four minutes, the person you've met will likely assume everything you do is positive. Within a mere ten seconds, that person will begin to make judgments about your professionalism, social class, character, morals, and intelligence.

Your speaking skills are judged also. Most employers believe that those who speak as if they care about their diction are more likely to care about their jobs. Even though we want to be judged by what's inside, outer appearance and diction form first impressions.

Not only is your voice a tool for conveying messages, your eyes dictate how serious you are when you communicate. Studies have shown that if your eye contact is consistent, you are perceived as more alert, confident, serious, dependable, and responsible.

Why is diction important? Your potential employer is looking at whom she would like to have as a representative in the company. A confident command of the language wins every time. Whether applying to a computer company or a fast food restaurant, put your best foot forward. People almost always outnumber available jobs: therefore you should practice your speaking skills with a tape or digital recorder or with a friend who has a better mastery of the language than you. In metropolitan areas, there are also centers that specialize in the improvement of speaking skills. Employed at such centers are speech pathologists, therapists, and phonologists. Many specialists strongly advocate the use of mainstream American English to avoid economic exploitation, exclusion, and unemployment. The consultant's function is to aid the speaker in areas including word pronunciation (phonology), hearing, tongue and lip positioning, diction, and timing.

Employers seek articulate people to fill management and sales positions. Correction can be a pleasant warning and not always a motive of discrimination. Although seemingly unfair, an employer may eliminate applicants due to poor speech patterns, preferring someone who can increase the sales of their product. Most employers perceive that speech is related to intelligence and social background. Generally, one who has a solid wherewithal with the language can be an asset to the company: a win/win situation for both parties.

When in doubt about how to use a word or phrase, save the embarrassing moment by asking a question. Pajamas and shorts are comfortable forms of clothing but that doesn't give everyone the liberty to wear them everywhere. In formal conversations, use Standard American English and trade the pajamas for business attire.

Try not to fall into the trap of actually thinking that you are a "sell-out" suffering from identity loss just because you may sound "proper" to some people. This is one of the oldest and most successful divide and conquer schemes ever implemented. This tactic is so ingrained into Black Americans' minds that we actually believe there is something wrong with sounding articulate. Many African Americans deduce that if whites do something, then it is evil or punishable to African Americans; which assumes that if whites are literate, literacy must be evil. Wayne Aponte expresses his disgust with Blacks who ridicule others for "talking white." He states, "Hearing the laughter and being the butt of 'proper' and 'Oreo' jokes hurt me. Being criticized made me feel marginal and verbally impotent in the sense that I had little ammunition to stop the frequent lunchtime attacks." The negative behavior Blacks perform against Blacks is not a by-product but a direct descendent of slavery. Increasing the ability to read will liberate, not enslave. Strong, intelligent Africans were flogged, tortured, and killed if they "got out of their place" and to this day, we still think that a Black person with certain skills is being defiant or uppity. Encourage someone who is trying to excel; do not place restrictions on their articulation. When in environments that call for intimacy amongst those who are cognizant of the dialect, talk as you wish. You should ensure that you don't lose that Black English touch in the 'hood. But in the classroom, conform for the grade. In the business world, conform to be understood.

Don't forget that the bottom line is being employed. The better the speaking skills, the greater your chances are at having the job of choice. Treat this as a rule because we must learn *mainstream English* to best position ourselves. "Communication is a key to mobility in any company or industry," says Howard H. Bond. The ability to communicate is not an option; it is mandatory.

Millions of Americans are suffering from what journalist Arnold Kemp called *genopsycholinguisticide*, a form of discrimination hidden deep within the obvious context of race, gender, socio-economic background, and appearance. It doesn't care about you. It only respects those who have adequate facility with what is commonly known as Standard American English. It also encourages the inferiority complex ensconced in Blacks. Who are the victims? Citizens who defy the unwritten law of the land: the ability and choice to read, write, speak, and understand the language of power and finance.

It has been estimated that over 14% of the United States population is functionally illiterate. This high rate of illiteracy nearly guarantees academic failure in high school and college. Education beyond high school does not guarantee a better society, but it gives us the opportunity to improve upon it.

Because language skills aren't stressed enough in the primary years, the adult suffers later in life. Elementary school teachers must challenge the system by not allowing administrative and parental bullying. We must stress that the blue-collar world has gone high tech, as well, which means that manual labor also requires literacy and more technical information. Vanishing employment has many euphemisms such as downsizing, outsourcing, and corporate outplacement, which are synonyms created to reduce stress on the fired employee.

Many of the shifts in recent years have been due to different realms of literacy. Computer, cultural, and corporate literacy are among the few forms that have dominated throughout the last decade, but oddly enough, the most basic and fundamental forms of literacy have been ignored: reading, writing, and speaking as they relate to good grammar and intonation.

Thousands of Americans are counted out of opportunities for something as simple as what one learns shortly after birth, if not before. Communication is a device used to encode and decode messages and to achieve your desires, but so many people don't realize how crucial each verbal situation can be.

Jencks and Phillips argue that an ordinary child in a predominantly black school is more likely to be in a larger class (in a school with a higher proportion of special needs children) receiving less attention from a less skilled teacher. This can lead to the following. For SAT scoring, the data shows that the average score for Blacks on the reading and writing sections of the test was 19% lower than whites. Richard Reeves points out the analysis of math data for college-bound seniors, finding very large racial achievement gaps. He says Blacks and Latinos remain clustered at the very bottom of the distribution. Blacks in particular lag far behind, with an average math score 31% lower than for Asians and 20% lower than whites, according to the College Board.

What's more, the Blacks tested were all born in the United States. African American math scores suffer due to the mainstream syntax and vocabulary used in story problems. In comparison to other ethnic groups, low scores amongst African Americans give admissions directors a perfect excuse to deny admission.

Attrition rates of African-Americans attending majority White campuses can be as high as 50%, with many quitting school within the first semester. African-American illiteracy can be as high as 75% in some major metropolitan areas, not just due to poor students, parents, and negative attitudes, but because many of the teachers and administrators choose to pass a student without adequate preparation for the next grade The social promotion assembly line will only create a collapse in society. Several studies have correlated illiteracy rates with crime and poverty. Becoming literate is not only a right, or privilege; it is a responsibility.

In later chapters, some terms and rules of grammar aren't recognized as incorrect; therefore studying the glossary should help with your speaking and writing skills.

MY EBONICS STORY

I was destined to become a professor, talk show host, and researcher. I was always surrounded by books in the home. Our parents had high standards, stressed education, and made sure that we had access to information.

As a youngster, my father coached me. Not only in sports, but he acted as a speech coach when I was 7 years old. Each day after work, he would roll out his Wollensak 3M reel-to-reel recorder and microphone. I didn't always like it but he would have a series of difficult words for me to pronounce. Meticulously, I would speak the words into the microphone while the reels would spin. Word after word, until tired, he would drill me on nouns, verbs, adjectives, compound words, and words with over 10 letters. I got better each day and my confidence level began to swell.

He made it a point of emphasis for me to speak clearly, rounding R's, hitting my "ing's," and following through on enunciation and stressing volume and inflection. He stressed that every word out of my mouth would be judged for content and aesthetic. He told me that being Black will amplify the ignorance of others, and how others will perceive your intelligence as luck or defiance. He told me to never create an excuse for someone to dismiss you with the mispronunciation of a word. My father only wanted what was best for his three boys. He wanted us to be able to walk through the landmines without causing explosions. He wanted us to know that being a Black male was always a reason for others to tease you, erase you, assume you were an athlete only, and consider you the antithesis of intelligent. My father wanted to ensure that we saw words as tools, weapons, healing agents, systems of offense, defense, and ways to navigate through precarious situations. He made sure that we knew that our Black lives mattered.

My mother maintained a close relationship with my teachers and was an active part of the PTA. She wouldn't allow any excuses for teachers to limit me, nor would she have a tolerance for me limiting myself.

When I was in the 5th grade, I suffered a severe blow to my ego. Knowing that I was the best speller in Indiana, I lost a spelling bee that felt like a punch in the gut. Missing a word that was quite simple, my world crumbled beneath my feet when the next speller commanded the word, proceeded to correctly spell the following one, and win the bee. Lesson learned.

My mother asked me if I wanted to win the bee next year. Of course I wanted to win. She then ushered a challenge to me by giving me a Webster's dictionary, an Oxford dictionary, and a purple spiral bound notebook. She told me to start from the beginning of both dictionaries and write every word that I didn't know. That summer was painstakingly horrible. Word after word, I wrote and studied so I couldn't be tripped up in the next school year's spelling bee. After accumulating more data than any 5th grader should, I won the spelling bee the following year. Mission accomplished.

I am eternally grateful to my parents for these valuable lessons. When parents warn you of potential pitfalls, it makes life a bit easier. In some Black communities where language is not stressed, we need teachers who care enough to correct students' English so test bias, test scores, and limited English proficiency don't continue to be significant factors to Black children.

THE GLOSSARY OF FORBIDDEN WORDS, DEFINITIONS, PHRASES, AND PRONUNCIATIONS

Ax or Ask?
Ask means "to call for an answer." Many pronounce this word with the "s" and "k" inverted, pronouncing the word incorrectly as "aks" or "ax." The correct pronunciation places the "s" before the "k" as in the words *task, bask, flask, and mask*. Archaic Tindel translations of older books spell this as *axeth*. During slavery, many words were changed in spelling and in pronunciation. With many Africans and some southern whites devoid of these alterations, language changes among us didn't always follow; therefore even today some expressions aren't pronounced according to what is considered Standard English. *Axeth* is outdated.

Abandon
Some say *abannon*. Be sure to include the *d* in abandon.

Abominable   (uh-bah-meh-nuh-bel)
The word means *detestable*. Nearly everyone has problems with words like this. Say it slowly..

Accidentally
Not *accidently*.

Aggravate/Irritate
Aggravate means "to make worse." You cannot aggravate something that isn't already bad. *Irritate* means "to annoy."

Ain't
Ain't is a *verb form*, colloquial contraction meaning *isn't* or expressing a negative (am not, is not). This should never be used in formal speech or writing. *Ain't* is often used in conversation and is rarely written, but during a job interview you shouldn't make use of the word.
Informal: This *ain't* the way to Chicago.
Formal: This *is not* the way to Chicago.

Alphabet (al-fuh-bet)   Album (al-bum)
Alcohol (al-co-hall)   Algebra (al-juh-bruh)
These can be very annoying words because many say the words without pronouncing the *l* in them.

Aluminum (al-loo-min-num)
There is only one *n* in aluminum. Be sure not to put 2 *n*'s around the *m*. Some say "aluminin" or "alunimun." You *can* really sound illiterate if you don't pronounce this with care.

Alzheimer's Disease
Named for Aloysius "Alois" Alzheimer, a German psychiatrist and neuropathologist, Alzheimer's Disease links symptoms to microscopic brain changes. Sadly, the scientist's name is

mispronounced in several ways. "All-timers," "Old-timers," and "Auld ang zymers" disease are just a few ways to say Alzheimer's incorrectly. See pronunciations - ahlts-hy-merz, alts-hy-merz, awlts-hy-merz.

a.m. (ante meridiem)
Abbreviation for *before noon*. Saying something twice can be an honest mistake but try to avoid this redundant devil. If you say "5 in the morning," this is acceptable. But if you say "5 *a.m.* in the morning," this is redundant because *a.m.* already implies morning.

Ambulance (am-byoo-lens /am-byoo-lance)
Many pronounce this word in the way they have heard it said around the house. Some pronounce it *am-bah-lance, ampa-lans,* and *ammuh'lams.* Both ways are incorrect and the person who is unsure should correct the pronunciation before using in an interview. It would be a shame to apply for a job at the hospital and not be able to pronounce *ambulance* correctly.

Amen (ay-men) (ah-men)
In no way am I going to try to attempt to change the way Black people say this word, especially in church during a good sermon. The word should be pronounced (ay-men) or (ah-men) with the second syllable as men, *not* "man." Commonly mispronounced "ay-man" but incorrect nevertheless.

Among/Between
Generally, when more than two things or more than two people are involved, the word *among* is used. *Between* is used when referring to two objects or things.

The following sentences are incorrect. *Tyrone couldn't choose between the three desserts. Julia saw me among one lady.* The following sentences are correct. *Tyrone couldn't choose from the three desserts. Julia saw me among three ladies.*

Answer

Do not cut off the letter *r* at the end of the word *answer*. Some say "ansuh" and this can be difficult to understand. Also do *not* pronounce the *w*.

Anxious (aink-shus)

Please do not mistake *anxious* for *eager*. Eager means "having keen desire or longing" whereas anxious means "full of anxiety, worried." The following examples are correct. "I was *eager* to see my best friend. I was *anxious* to see my bad report card."

Aunt (awnt)

Do not say "auntie," or "awntie," in a formal situation. Feel free to use these at home or with friends. In formal speech, think before you say "awntie." Pronouncing as "ant" is also acceptable.

Authentic

Pronounce the last *t* in authentic.. Do not cut off by saying "awthennick." Cutting letters off words can covertly suggest that you're lazy and careless in your speech.

Bad

Bad meaning bad, or *bad* meaning good? This word can be tricky in many conversations that require accuracy. *Bad* meaning "good" is slang and should be avoided if around unfamiliar people.

Band
Articulate the *d* at the end of the word. It's easy to cut it off in a sentence. *Sand* is similar.

Band-Aid/bandage
Band-Aid is a product name of bandages. Don't confuse the brand name with the product. A bandage is something used to protect an open sore or cut.

Barbed Wire
Some say "bob wire" or "bobbed wire." *Barbed wire* is correct.

Bathroom/Birthday
Pronounce *th* in both words. Many people put an *f* sound in there making the words sound like this: baf-room and birf-day. No! Many times this pronunciation is due to association. What is heard in the home and in the peer group can be incorrect.

Be
The verb *"be"* has always been used creatively in the Black community. Black people have creatively changed the use of the *"be"* verb, by saying "he be, we be, you be." When you're with your peer group, feel free to use it how you choose. But in formal environments, be careful. "We be going to the store after we get paid," is incorrect. A correct examples would be, "We are going to the store after we get paid." The *be* verbs are *be, am, is, are, was, were, been,* and *being.*

Beach/Beech
If you misspell one of these words, you will confuse your reader. A

beach is a pebbly or sandy shore, but a *beech* is a forest tree with smooth bark and glossy leaves.

Believed
Do not say believe-did, as in *I believe-did her.* Similar to *skinded for skinned* and *look-tid for looked.*

Between you and I
Between you and me is proper.

Blessing in disguise or a blessing in the skies
A *blessing in disguise* is the proper phrase. It means that something good has happened and it was not readily or overtly expected or exposed. A *blessing in the skies* is what some people say, but this is not the correct expression, unless you mean that the blessing actually comes from the sky. To be safe, use the first phrase.

Break/Brake
Don't confuse these words. Two different meanings and spellings occur here. *Break* means to separate into pieces under blow or strain, shatter or disconnect to make inoperative. *Brake* means a device for stopping motion of a wheel or vehicle.

Breath
Here is another word mispronounced by many people. The "th" at the end of the word is pronounced by placing the tongue gently against the back of the upper front teeth before articulation. This ensures the "th" sound. Some people may pronounce this as "bref,"

but "bref" requires the upper front teeth to be on the bottom lip. This action shouldn't occur while saying this word.

Brought/Bought

The verbs *bring* and *buy* are often confused. You must make it a point to think before speaking when using these words. The past tense for *bring* is *brought*. The past tense for *buy* is *bought*. The following examples are incorrect. "I *brought* the bicycle from the salesperson for one hundred dollars. I *bought* this game from home." These are correct. "I *bought* the bicycle from the salesperson for one hundred dollars. I *brought* this game from home."

Buffet

Buffet has a silent "t" at the end. It is pronounced (buf-fay) not (buf-fett). This pertains to meals or food bought in a line without service. *Buffet* has a French origin and a French pronunciation (silent "t"). Warren Buffett's name has two *t*'s and the sound is pronounced.

Business

Business does not have a *d* sound. Those of you who say *bid-ness* know who you are.

Busted/Burst/Bursted/Bust

All are incorrect. The correct form that should be used is the word *burst*. *Burst* should be used in the past, present, future, and past participle forms. *Yesterday the balloon burst. Today the balloon burst. Tomorrow the balloon will burst.*

Calendar/Calender

Calendar with an "a" at the end is what we use for dates (month, year). *Calender* with an "e" at the end is a machine for rolling cloth or paper. They have similar pronunciations so watch your spelling. This is an excusable mistake.

Calvary and Cavalry

Watch the position of letters. You don't want to switch pronunciation for two very important words.

Can I, May I

Can denotes ability. *May* represents permission. Don't confuse the two. Examples of proper use are found here.
Can I jump higher than him?
May I have some cookies and cake?

Candidate

Pronounce both *d*'s in candidate. Some speakers say "cannadit."

Certificate (ser-ti-fi-kit)

I've heard this word said in many ways from *susificate* to *certifisus*. Actually it is a simple four-syllable word but saying it slowly is probably the best measure for saying it correctly.

Children

Many times mispronounced as *chiwdren, chilren, chillin, sheerin*. The word *children* has an "l" and a "d" that need to be pronounced in formal situations.

Colloquialism (everyday speech)

Colloquialisms, slang phrases, and jargon should be avoided in some formal situations. Colloquialism can easily offend people or exclude them from conversation. However, if the situation calls for a looser structure, feel free to interject colloquialisms. Once you become more familiar with an individual or group, some parts of everyday speech are allowed.

Colorado or Codorado

Some say *Codorado*, removing the *l*. Keep the *l* in there.

Confide/Confine

These words have different meanings. To express that you've confided in someone is one thing, but to confine someone is another. *Confide* is to tell a secret or to entrust. *Confine* is to keep or restrict.

Confusable words in Black English

As understood by listener	Intended word
ball	boil
coal	cold
dough	door
guess	guest
jaw	jar
hole	hold
pitcher	picture

rat   right
show   sure
win   wind
send   sin

Consonant Cluster Deletion

Some African Americans pronounce the following words with a consonant deleted. Pronounce the final or post-vocalic consonants in the words below: fac (fact), lif (lift), tes (test), fin (find), col (cold), lis (list), hans (hands).

Cope

This word is an intransitive verb used with the word "with." In formal writing, one doesn't *cope* but one *copes with* something or somebody. Informal: *Gladys coped.* Formal: *Gladys coped with the terrible situation.*

Copyright

Contrary to belief, there is no such word as *copywritten*. A *copyright* is a legal document that proves that a person owns the rights to a work. The past tense for *copyright* is *copyrighted*, not copywritten.

Cordoroys

Clothing made from twisted fibers is called *corduroy*. But some say cordurod, codorod, ca-dew-rod, co-lo-roy, and co-do-row.

Crib/House

If you ever make this mistake in a formal situation, you better laugh it off, or say the word *house* as quickly as you can. Generally this term is a regional one, but say *house* instead of *crib*. Slang terms are fine around friends, but in changing environments, use the predominant language of the environs. *Crib* also has some negative historic connotations. Some sociologists believe that some Black men use this word to express his diminutive status in terms of ownership (Blacks being able to own *cribs*, but not big houses). Some also think that this is linked with many Blacks referring to their friends as "babies" (as in, "what's up, baby?") and referring to Caucasian men as "the man." I have reservations about origins, but theory may feasibility. Nevertheless, use house or home instead of crib.

Daughter

Careful not to say dor-ter or dor-der.

Decathlon, Heptathlon, Triathlon

There is no vowel sound between the *th* and *l*. Some are inclined to add the syllable but it doesn't exist.

Dial (dy-el)

With this word, pronunciation is very important because someone may interpret your saying of *dial* as something else. Don't cut the "l" off of the word. Good pronunciation is simply the articulation of every syllable and every letter that should be pronounced. I've heard this pronounced *"die,"* *"di'uh,"* and *"doll."*

Dilate or Dialate
No such word as *dialate*. The word is *dilate*.

Dis
Dis as a colloquial expression means to discount or disrespect. One can make this word invention sound formal depending on how the word is delivered but avoiding this word would be advisable. Some pronounce "this" as "dis" too. You may get "dissed" in a job interview if you use "dis."

Doberman Pinscher
It's not "Domomann" or "Dobo mann" pinscher. The correct way to say it is (Doe-ber-man). Children in the neighborhood destroy this pronunciation. Let's teach them the right way to say it. *Pinscher* is pronounced (pin-schur).

Door
Pronounce "r" at the end. Do not say "doe."

Double Negatives
Two negatives in a sentence should not be used together. Many African Americans love double negatives so be careful in formal speech. Avoid the following. *I ain't got none. We*

don't have no money. You can easily correct these by saying or writing: *I don't have any. I have none.*

Drawers
Pronounced (draw-ers), this is a word for items that go in dressers and an alternative word for underwear. Colloquially, this is said in the Black community as "draws." Please say briefs or drawers in mixed company or else somebody may not have any idea what you're talking about.

Drowned (drown'd)
Similar to *skinned,* drowned is not pronounced with the extra "did" on the end: drowned (drown'd), not drowndid.

Enthusiasm
Be very careful not to say *enthused.* The formal word is *enthusiasm.* In everyday talk, people will say *enthuse* but this is not Standard American English. Say the entire word in order to avoid confusion.
Informal: I was *enthused* when I heard the good news.
Formal: I was *enthusiastic* when I heard the good news.

Enunciation and Pronunciation
Enunciation is the act of pronouncing words. The way in which a word is *pronounced is pronunciation.*

Escape or Excape or Xscape or Exscape
Escape is the correct spelling. No *ex* or *x* in escape.

Espresso or Expresso
Many pronounce *espresso* as *expresso*. If you drink too much espresso, you may make the mistake of saying *expresso*. Get *cafe' au lait* instead.

Et cetera (et-set-er-uh)
Etc. or *et cetera* means "and other things." Please delete it from your written works. It is often over used in speech as well.

Expect/Suspect
The words *expect* and *suspect* differ. *Expect* is the assumption of a future event. *Suspect* means to be inclined to think (of, that); mentally accuse of; as a noun it means a person who has been accused, or has the potential of being accused. I *expect* Eugene to be here at 8:00 p.m. I *suspect* that Jeffrey has taken my train set.

Experience
Do not cut off any syllables or letters in this word. Pronounce *eks-peer-ee-ence*. Some mispronounce this one (ex-spince).

February
February has 2 (two) "r's" in it so pronounce them both. Do

not say *Febuary*. The second syllable, *bru*, is pronounced like it is spelled. Phonetically, the word would be pronounced: Feh-brew-air-eee. Feh (eh sound as in leg), Brew (u sound as in you), Air (as in Air Force Ones), E (as in squeak).

Fellows
Pronounced like *bellow* or *mellow*. This word isn't exclusive to the Black community but in a formal situation say *fellows*, not *fell-uz*.

Fensta/Finsta
See Fixin.'

Film
Many of us say *fim*, while forgetting the *"l"* that is pronounced in the middle of the word. I have also heard this word pronounced *fil-um*. The words *pattern* and *film* have consonants at the end. Do not place vowel sounds between these consonants. See *pattern*.

Fixin'
Strunk and White's, *The Elements of Style*, shows how this term can be abused in a few ways. Some Blacks often add to the complexity of this word by saying the phrase, *fixin to* or *finnah* This means "to get ready" and falls in line with the colloquial meaning for the word, *to arrange, to prepare,* or *to mend,* but the word is from *figere* which means "to make

firm," or "to place definitely." An example of this usage would be: *I'm fixin' to go to the store.* Try this: *I'm preparing (or: getting ready) to go to the store.* Be very careful with words and phrases you've grown up with around your house and neighborhood. Using these words can cause a negative response in a professional or academic environment.

Flesh/Flush
Don't confuse these. If you say, "He my flush and blood" not only do you have a missing verb, but you also have a vowel incorrectly pronounced. Flesh is with an "e."

For all intents and purposes or For all intensive purposes
Nearly every person I hear butchers this expression. For all intents and purposes is a legal term used in court and on contracts. Sadly, outside of court people say, "intensive." Stick to the legal phrase.

Found
There is no *t* sound at the end of this word. Do not say *fount.* A "d" sound is present at the end of *found.*

Freeze/Squeeze
These two words can be very confusing in the past tense and past participle. Use freeze, froze, frozen...squeezed, squeezed, squeezed. There are no such words as *squezzed, squozen, frozed* or *frozened.*

Frontwards
This is a terrible substitute for forward.

Fruit
The letter 'r' loses its vocality more than other consonants. Because of an impediment or environment, some people may never learn how to pronounce the word 'fruit.' Have you ever heard someone say "fewt" or "fwoot"? The 'r' is lost in the mix. Strangely enough, a person mispronouncing fruit may not have problems pronouncing the 'r' in other words, such as *run* or *rest*. Consult a speech pathologist if you have problems with consonant clusters.

Frustrated (mispronounced "flustrated")
Do not place the letter "l" in the word *frustrated*. It does not have an "l" in it and its first syllable is "frus," not "flus." The correction may be frustrating but with practice, a speaker should be able to pronounce the word correctly.

Go
Present tense: go   Past tense: went   Past Participle: gone

Good/Well
These are tricky words. Many still have problems with these words but if you follow the rule, you will not stumble. Here's the rule: *Good* is an adjective and often follows a linking verb. Example: The silk scarf feels *good*.

Well is an adverb and often follows an action verb. However, when *well* means "in good health," "attractive," or "satisfactory," it is used as an adjective.

I work *well* in the morning. [adverb]
Christina doesn't feel *well*. [adjective --- "in good health"]

Government
Not only exclusive to the Black community but a word that should be articulated properly. Many tend to say *guv'ment* or *guvva'ment,* deleting the "vern" in the middle of the word.

Granted or Granite
Take something for *granted*, not for *granite* - unless you have a lift truck with good shocks.

Grasshopper/Firefly/Beetle
Above you will see the correct words for our friends in the insect world. Sometimes *grasshopper* is inverted and pronounced *hoppergrass*. As a child I used to always use the colloquial form for *firefly* which is *lightning bug*. I also used the expression *pinching bug* and you should simply say *beetle*. These aren't that crucial in everyday speech, but try to adapt when possible.

Gray Areas

Some words have been accepted into mainstream English. Such words are blimp, blizzard, flabbergast, gadget, jazz, ogle, quiz, and snob - *Elements of Style*. The acceptance and rejection of some words can be racist. Words like *dope, fly, magnet, bond,* and *large* are looked upon with scorn because their origins stem from the Black community. What is the difference in saying, "That Lexus is cool" or "That Lexus is bond"? The latter expression is actually less abstract because it pertains to value. *Cool* refers to temperature, which has nothing to do with its value or description. But depending upon context, something considered *cool* is given a greater value. You will have to judge this by your interaction with others, formally and informally. A gray area would allow a term of jargon or slang to be used informally if both are aware and comfortable with the term. There are certain common phrases that are acceptable because the majority of the speaking society is familiar with the phrase. Keep speech simple for clarity.

Grow

There is no such word as growed as in "growed up."
Present: grow   Past: grew   Past Participle: have grown

Gwynne

This is another way of saying the word *going*. *Gwynne* is seen in slave narratives, late 19th and early 20th century novels, and it is heard in speech by those in the south who adhere to Black Vernacular and Southern dialect from earlier years. Delete from formal speech. *I's gwynne to the store.* This sentence should be replaced with this statement. I am *going* to the store.

Hanged/Hung
People are hanged; objects are hung. Hence, you should not say: *The penalty for the criminal was for him to be hung.* Since people are *hanged,* you must say: *The penalty for the criminal was for him to be hanged.* If you are referring to a picture on the wall, you should say: *I hung the picture on the wall.*

Height and Heighth
No such word as *heighth* (with a "th" at end). Breadth, depth, width, and length are valid. No such word as heighth. The word is height.

Heimlich manuever not Heineken remover
First aid abdominal thrusts used to clear upper airway obstructions or choking by foreign objects are often called the *Heimlich maneuver.* The term is named after Dr. Henry Heimlich. Do not mispronounce as the *Heineken remover.* This is the disappearance of a beverage.

Hierarchy
The word has four syllables, not three. Some say hi-archy, but the word sounds like "higher-arkee."

Hisself
This is non-standard for *himself*.

Homonyms
Homonyms are words that look alike or sound alike but have different meanings. Be sure not to confuse words because of their homonymic structure. Two examples are *some/sum* and *sun/son*. Though the words in each sound alike, their definitions differ. Be careful not to misspell.

Humiliate/Humility
Humiliate means to harm the dignity or self-respect of someone. *Humility* means to have a humble attitude. Do not confuse the two.

Hundred (hun-dred)
You must be careful of pronunciation. It is a two syllable word. Many make the mistake of saying, "Give me a *hunnerd* dollars. Give me a *hunna* dollars."

Hurt
There is no such word as hurted.
Present: hurt   Past tense: hurt   Past: have hurt

Ignorant (ig-nuh-rent) (ig-nor-ent)
A three syllable word, not a two syllable. Do not pronounce (ig-nent) or (ig-na-nent) because you will sound ignorant.

Illinois
Do not pronounce the "s" because this state maintains a silent consonant.

Interested
Interested has the suffix "inter" in it. The lazy tongue says "intrested." Slow down and say "in-ter-es-ted."

Interpret or Interpretate
To explain the meaning of a word or sentence is to *interpret*. There is no such word as *interpretate*, or *conversate*. An interpretation is the action of explaining the meaning of something.

Irregardless/Regardless
Regardless means without regard or consideration, therefore, *irregardless* is a double negative. *Regardless* is saying without regard; *irregardless* is saying without no regard, hence the double negative. Make it easy on yourself and say *regardless*. The word *irregardless* is not standard and is erroneous.

Iron
Pronounced (i'urn). Oh haven't you heard many of us pronounce this word as a one syllable word (arn)? It does have two syllables so say them both, (eye-urn) or (eye-ern).

Jewelry
Jewelry is not pronounced "jury" or "jew-ry." The "l" is pronounced. Try saying it slowly with the following phonetic pronunciations (jew-well-ree), (jewel-ry).

Kindergarten
The mispronunciation of *kindergarten* is painful to my ears. I've seen many children who cannot pronounce the grade in school that they are currently attending. How many parents and children have constantly said "kenny-garden" or "kinna-garden"? Speech starts at a young age and we must take care in teaching the child. How can we expect our children to be articulate if we don't reinforce spelling, diction, and what is appropriate in the home?

Laboratory
Be sure to pronounce the 'r' sounds. It is more comfortable to drop the middle 'r' and say "labatory" but this will hint laziness.

Laptop or Labtop
A *laptop* computer is for your lap, not your lab. Be precise

with your pronunciation.

Lackadaisical

It means *unenthusiastic*. This word's first syllable is pronounced *lack*, not *lax* or lacks. Though it's somewhat related to the word *lax* and *laxity* it is not pronounced like them. *Lack-eh-day-zih-kel* isn't a hard word to pronounce, though many have heard it incorrectly pronounced, therefore perpetuating the mispronunciation.

Learn/Teach

Learn is something a student does. *Teach* is what the instructor does. Informal: *Learn me how to play the guitar.* Formal: *Teach me how to play the guitar.*

Leave/Let

Leave and *let* are abused on a number of occasions. I've seen these words tortured in speech.
Incorrect: *Leave* the children play in the park.
Correct: *Let* the children play in the park.
Incorrect: *Let* him alone.
Correct: *Leave* him alone.

Libel and Liable

Don't confuse *libel* and *liable*. *Libel* means false publication that damages a person's reputation *Liable* means legally responsible.

Library/Libary
Laziness can rid the best speaker of credibility. Library has the letter "r" in it twice.

Liquid Consonants
These are consonants not pronounced due to an overriding emphasis on the final consonant or vowel: hep (help), faught (fault), toe (toll).

Live/Live
Two pronunciations are here. One has a short "i" sound as in (liv) and the other a long "i" as in (lyv).

Loan/Lend/Borrow
Loan is a noun. When using verb tense, one should use *lend*. When using nouns as verbs, you can confuse the listener. The following are not appropriate: *Borrow me a dollar. Loan me a dollar.* But the following sentence, with the verb replacement would be fine. *Lend me twenty dollars.*

Looked (look-t)
Looked is a word similar to *skinned* in its pronunciation. Be careful not to say (look-tid). Yes indeed, you have definitely heard Black children and adults say "looktid" as in, "That girl look-tid good!"

Lost / Loss

Lost is the past tense for *to lose*. Loss is something denotes an absence, but please do not say "I'm sorry for your lost." Use the word *loss* for condolences.

Mayonnaise

The word has three syllables. Some pronounce it "man-ays."

Miniature or Miniture

There is an "a" in *miniature*. Please pronounce it.

Minneapolis and Indianapolis

Tricky, tricky, tricky! Sound out the letters and syllables in these two big cities and you should be able to eliminate your pronunciation problem. Never say the words too fast. Do not put an extra syllable and *nap* in Minneapolis. *Connecticut* and Massachusetts are two more tough ones.

Misconfused

No such word as *misconfused*. Fascinating pronunciation, but this may be a hybrid of confused and misunderstood.

Misunderestimate

Say *underestimate*, not *misunderestimate*.

Modern

Modern has two syllables, not three. Do not say "mo-der-in."

See *pattern and southern.*

Month
There is no "f" in *month.*

Mute and Moot
Be careful. *Mute* is the absence of speech or sound. *Moot* is subject to debate, uncertainty, or dispute.

Names of Writers and Artists
I have an anecdote pertaining to this category. I was in a bookstore one day and a young lady tried to impress me with her words. I walked to the counter with a stack of books to purchase and we started talking about writers. First we mentioned some contemporaries and then we ventured into history. Out of the blue, she mentions Albert Camus. This was fine but she didn't have a clue on how to say the author's name correctly. Communication served its purpose because I knew who Camus was, but her pronunciation was a disaster. The "s" that ends Albert Camus is a silent one and she pronounced that "s" over and over. By this time, I was driven right up the wall. Later she mentioned another writer, Dostoevsky, and needless to say, I was "too through." After I politely corrected her, we still continued our discussion. It was a tragedy to see this 34 year old Black woman mispronounce these words, but it proves that we can all learn something everyday, despite age or education.

Ax or Ask? The African American Guide to Better English

Nan

Nan is an expression that means "none." Often used in conjunction with "one," this word should not be used at all in formal situations. Informal: *I don't want nan one of them men because they ain't makin' no money.* This is a better way to say the above thought. Formal: *I don't want any of those men because they don't earn enough money.*

Nauseous/Nauseated

The first means "sickening to contemplate;" the second means "sick to the stomach." Do not say "I feel nauseous," unless you are sure you have that effect on others (Strunk & White -- The Elements of Style).

Naw

Informal substitute for *no*.

The "N" Word

Nobody in the world should use this term. In some parts of England, the word is punishable. It's too bad it's not punishable in the United States. The term is a derogatory term referring to Africans. In Anthony T. Browder's book, *From the Browder Files*, Browder tells us that it derives from *necro*, which means dead. Negro means black and comes from the Spanish definition which isn't so bad. The reality is that the word *n*.... was created to degrade and to sub humanize Africans in the middle passage and in slavery. The sad end to the story is that we as a people use it on each other to degrade and to compliment. *Release this burden from your vocabulary. Necro,* to *Negro,* to *n...* What an evolution? And you ask, what's in a name? Plenty! Julianne Malveaux stated in Essence Magazine, "Don't call me a n....." Just between us Black folks, the word n.... is often used as a term of endearment. As our society becomes more superficiality integrated, others pick up the term because they hear us use it among ourselves. If we want other people to stop using this derisive slur, then we need to make sure we stop using it ourselves."

Nuclear or Nucular
Watch the metathesis here. Avoid the George W. Bush pronunciation.

Numbers
Enunciate numbers with crisp consonants. It is easy to get into the habit of saying, *foe* instead of *four, fi* instead of *five,* and *naan* instead of *nine.* Functional pronunciation and literacy is important in situations outside of our community.

Nuptial / Nuptual
Nuptial pertains to a wedding. *Nuptual* is not a word.

Oil
Oil has regional pronunciations. The great midwestern dialect

has this pronunciation (oy-el). in some regions, it is pronounced *all*, *arl*, and *erl* but for formal situations, safety would have us use the (oy-el) pronunciation.

Old/Ode
Old means with age surpassing that of others. Ode is a story or a poem written to be sung. You may here some people say, "He so *ode* his friends are Brutus and Caesar." Watch both grammar and the way words are pronounced.

Ordnance and Ordinance
Be careful with these words. *Ordnance* pertains to mounted guns; artillery. *Ordinance* pertains to a piece of legislation enacted by a municipal authority.

Orient or Orientate
No such word as *orientate*.

Pattern (pat'urn)
Pattern is pronounced (pa-turn); it is not pronounced (pat'er'in). It doesn't end with a third syllable (in). It has just two syllables.

Percolate or Perculate
It's time for the percolator. *Percolate* is a word. *Perculate* is not a word.

Perspire or Prespire
Perspire means to sweat through the pores. *Prespire* is not a word.

Picture
Pronounced (pick-chur), not pitcher.

Plurals
Watch closely for words that do not simply take an "s" to make them plural. Words like *leaf, shelf, and half,* change form when in the plural. *Leaf* becomes *leaves, shelf* becomes *shelves,* and *half* becomes *halves.* Be careful with the plural of men/women. Never say mens, unless it's possessive (men's).

Polish/polish
This word is pronounced two ways. Actually there are two different words here. One means to clean or buff something and to make smooth and glossy by rubbing. Its pronunciation is (pah-lish) with a short vowel sound. The other is Polish as in the country of Poland; of or relating to Polska. It's pronounced (poh-lish) with a long "o."

Poor
Pronounced *poor* not po.'

Prerogative over Perogative

Bobby Brown would say it's his *prerogative* which is correct. The word starts with *pre* not *per*.

Probably

Don't forget the "b." It's easier and more efficient to say *prolly*, but that pronunciation is informal.

Prostate and Prostrate

Do not confuse the two. *Prostate* is part of a man's anatomy. *Prostrate* is lying stretched out on the ground with one's face downward.

Psychology/Psalm/Psoriasis/Pneumonia

Though they all start with a "p" they do not have the "p" sound. The "p" is silent.

Quarter

Ahhh, I've heard this pronounced "quota" but it's (kwarter).

Quit

There is no such word as "quitted" for the past tense of quit.
Present: quit   Past: quit   Past Participle: have quit

Racial and Sexual Slurs
In the words of Malcolm X, please avoid racial and sexual slurs "by any means necessary." Slurs do not help anyone. Derogatory words are vehicles used to humiliate people, making them appear to be inferior or subhuman. Don't use these because it blatantly shows that you are a racist or sexist. Telling an ethnic joke displays a high level of intolerance, ignorance, and inequality. Words are powerful, so choose them wisely.

Read
This word has two different pronunciations. The present tense pronunciation has a long *ee* sound, but the past tense pronunciation sounds like the color.

Realtor
Do not add a syllable to *realtor*. Some say *realator (real-uh-tour)*, but incorrect.

Regular
Do not say "regulla."

Relevant (rel-uh-vent)
Do not switch the "v" and "l" or else you'll have the word *revelent*. *Rel* is the first syllable (not *rev*).

Reptile
The 'p' should be pronounced. Many say 'reh-tile' forgetting that the word has a vocal 'p.'

Respectively and Respectfully
Do not use interchangeably. *Respectively* deals with the order of something; *respectfully* deals with respect. See correct uses below.
> *I kissed my mother and girlfriend, respectively.* (order)
> *Respectfully, I bowed to the audience.* (respect)

Right Fast
An overused expression used in the Black community that is often said when referring to something happening quickly. Actually the word "momentarily" or the expression "in a moment" should be used. In some cases, the word *quickly* could be used to replace *right fast*. Informal: *Hold on right fast; I have a phone call. Wait right fast, I'm getting her address.* Formal: *Hold momentarily; I have another call. Wait a moment; I'm getting her address.* Try to eliminate *right fast* from your vocabulary because if you continue to use it in informal situations, you may use it in formal ones.

Sandwich
Please pronounce the "d," "w," and the "ch" in this word. It is very easy to say "sam-mich," "san-wich," and "san-mich" instead of *sand-wich*.

Scared
Some people pronounce this word "scurd." Music videos and popular culture also reinforce this pronunciation, but you should stick to the formal: scared.

School/Scoo
Leaving the "l" off of school can lead to a spelling and reading problem later on. For emphasis, the *l* is left off in the Black community. Dr. Geneva Smitherman talks of this in her book *Black Talk*. A consonant after a vowel is a post-vocalic consonant. We also see this in the word *cool*.

Secretary
This word is another one that can lose its 'r' if said incorrectly, i.e: 'seckatary.'

See
Some people say, " I seed it" or "I seent it." You will get corrected or stared at for these.
Present tense: see
Future tense: will see
Past tense: saw
Past Participle: have seen

Separate
Spelling this word is difficult because the letter "a" appears in the middle. Not *seperate*, but *separate*.

Shake
Present: Shake   Past: Shook   Past Participle: Shaken

Sherbet
No Ernie or Bert after *sherbet*. Leave Bert on Sesame Street.

Shine
Shine has two definitions: 1) to glow, and 2) to polish. When it is used to describe glowing, the forms are shine, shone, shone. When used to describe polishing, the forms are shine, shined, shined.

Shrimp
Correct pronunciation: sh-rimp.
Here are African-American mispronunciations for shrimp: Scrimp, Squimp, Swemp, Swimp, Swaimpses

Silicon and Silicone
Silicon is a nonmetallic element found in the earth's crust. The element is a major component in semiconductors, and its high conductivity makes it useful in solar power cells. *Silicone* is a class of silicon-based chemical compounds used in paints, adhesives, lubricants, and implants.

Skinned
There is one "d" in this word. Say *skinned* not *skin-ded.* I still slip on this one from time to time. Be careful.

South

The "f" sound should not creep into your *south*. Like breath or shall I say "bref," some choose to use the "f" sound for south. The "th" is clear and you should use your tongue and your teeth for this sound.

Southern

Southern has two syllables (suh-thurn), not three as in "su-thur-in." The words *modern* and *pattern* also have two syllables.

Spay and Spade

Spay is to render a female mammal infertile. *Spade* is a small shovel or a playing card. Misspelling can be painful.

Statistic

This word is a tongue twister for many people. Slow your rate and it is easier to pronounce. Break it down to three syllables (sta-tis-tick). Practicing will do wonders.

Straight

Be careful not to pronounce this word with the "sk" sound as in "skrate." This colloquial pronunciation is acceptable in music videos and in casual conversation, but "skrate" should be avoided in formal conversations.

Strawberry or Skrawberry

This usually isn't a speech defect, but some pronounce "straw" as "skraw" with the "t" substituted as a "k." Be careful.

Strength

Strehn-th, not strumph.

Strong or Skrong

This usually isn't a speech defect, but some pronounce "strong" as "skrong" with the "t" substituted as a "k."

Subtle

In class, I've heard this pronounced "sub-tl." The "b" in *subtle* is so subtle you can't hear it. It is silent, therefore cut it. Pronounced *suttle*. *Subtle* means hard to detect or to describe.

Suburb

Suburb has one "r" in it. I've heard this pronounced "sur-burb" and "sub-ub."

Supposedly

Don't place the letter "b" in this one. It is (sup-po-sed-ly), not (sup-po-sub-ly).

Subject/Verb Agreement

Make sure that your subject always agrees with your verb. If you have a plural subject, your verb must match it or your sentence will sound awkward. Do not make these common mistakes.

The boys and girls plays the dozens. The boy play the piano.

These are the correct sentences.

The boys and girls play the dozens each day. The boy plays the piano.

Supremacist and Supremist

Spelled both ways but supremacist is usually the more formal of the two. Supremist is a lazier way of saying supremacist. Nothing could be worse than a lazy supremacist.

Sure

The "su" gives the word a "sh" sound as in "sugar." But many delete the "re" ending by pronouncing the word "sho" as in "sho you right" instead of "sure you're right."

Sweep
Present: sweep   Past: swept   Past Participle: swept

Swim
Present: swim   Past: swam   Past Participle: swum

Ax or Ask? The African American Guide to Better English

Swing
Present: swing   Past: swung   Past Participle: swung

Teach
Present: teach   Past: taught   Past Participle: have taught

Tear
Present: tear   Past: tore   Past Participle: torn

Temperature
Not tem-puh-cher.

Tenant or Tenet
A principle or belief, especially one of the main principles of a religion or philosophy is a *tenet*. A person who occupies land or property rented from a landlord is a *tenant*. Close in sound so enunciate.

Tests
The plural of test is tests. Be careful not to say "tessis."

Than/Then
Than is a statement of comparison. *Then* means "at that time," "after," "next." Examples: I am taller *than* you are. Since *then*, two motorists were injured on the curve.

The letter R...uh
When pronouncing the letter *R*, be careful not to vocalize the

additional syllable uh. No Q, R-uh, S - but Q, R, S.

Their/There/They're
These three are serious spelling demons. Because they sound similar, you must be careful not to miss these. *Their* signifies possession; *there* denotes location; and *they're* is the contraction for "they are."

Think
Not thunk or thank.
Present: think   Past: thought   Past Participle: have thought

Through
Pronounced: (throo). The "r" is important. Stop saying,"I'm thoo' arguin' witchu."

Throw
There is no such word as "throwed."
Present: throw   Past: threw   Past Participle: have thrown

To/Too/Two
All of these words sound alike but they have different definitions and spellings. Remember the homonyms we saw earlier? *To* introduces a noun or expresses what is reached; *too* means "to a greater extent than desirable or permissible;" *two* is a number.

Try and...

This expression is overused. *Try and make some money.* The action here is "trying to do" not "try and." The correct usage would be: *Try to make some money.*

Use to could

Avoid this expression and just say, "was once able," or "used to be able." This is a common expression among children. Incorrect: *I used to could beat you running.* Correct: *I used to be able to beat you running. I was once able to beat you running.*

Utmost or Upmost

I have the *utmost* respect if you don't use *upmost*. *Utmost* means highest and is a superlative. *Upmost* can be a shortened form of uppermost, but not commonly used.

Unique

We know we can use this word out of context. Often we are taught to say this word and use it out of its definition. The word cannot be comparative or superlative. It simply means "without like or equal," which means there aren't levels of unique. Incorrect: *His car is more unique than yours.*
To clean up the above sentence, we should take out the degree, as stated in the definition, and simply state that the car is *unique*. *Correct: His customized car is unique; yours is like the others.* This keeps the sentence simple also, and does

not allow you to get into a verbal war over whose vehicle is *more unique*. It is simply, *unique*.

Valentine's Day
Valentine is often mispronounced and misspelled Balentine's and Valentime's.

Verbiage or Verbage
"You talk too much homeboy you never shut up." RUN-DMC
Verbiage is the proper spelling. Don't mess with the "i." Verbiage means speech or writing that uses too many words or excessively technical expressions.

Washing
Often pronounced with an "r" sound (warshing), washing should be said without the "r" sound.

Wasn't and Wadn't
Wasn't is the contracted form of *was not*. Avoid wadn't.

Whole other - Whole another - Whole 'nother
All three terms are used for emphasis, but try to avoid. *Another* is adequate.

Wit/Wiff/With
With can be mispronounced in many ways. "Wit" and "wiff" are two ways to mispronounce "with" as "I'll get wit you later," and "Momma, take me to the store wiff you."

Woke - Stay Woke

In formal company, avoid the use of the term, *stay woke*. Use *awake* instead. The term is a so-called expression of having a higher consciousness than others. The term is acceptable in relaxed scenarios, but for the most part try to avoid. Remain awake and avoid *stay woke*.

Variations in Pronunciation

Words that make the English language complicated are vowel sounds with "strange and silent" letters in them. Here are a few examples. Through, bough, though, rough, and bought all have different pronunciations. But notice, their endings are alike. They all have the letters "ough" in them, but 5 ways of saying the syllable exist. *Through* has the (oo) sound. *Bough* has the (ow) sound. *Though* has the (oh) sound. *Rough* has the (uf) sound. *Bought* has the (awt) sound.

Vaseline

Vaseline is a product trademark for a company that makes petroleum jelly. All petroleum products aren't Vaseline. Don't use interchangeably.

Verb Removal

Sometimes verbs are removed to place greater emphasis or priority on a situation. One would say, "John tired" instead of "John is tired." Avoid in a formal situation.

Vigil - Visual

Keeping awake, watching, and praying are signs of a vigil. Seeing is visual. Do not confuse the pronunciation and definitions. *Prayer visual* is incorrect. *Prayer vigil* is correct

Vulgarity

In the privacy of some homes or amongst friends, vulgarities are sometimes allowed. But when in public, or with more sensitive individuals, you should try your best to avoid vulgarities at all costs. Please delete them from your public and formal vocabulary. "We can often make our point as emphatically by not cursing at all. For instance, you can make someone seem more slimy and dishonest when you call him a prevaricator than when you call him a liar with an [expletive]. Challenge yourself not to use foul language. Find a dictionary, a thesaurus, and a better set of adjectives!" Julianne Malveaux

Y'all

The truncated form for *you all* is *y'all*. The word "you" can be a singular or plural pronoun. Restrict to comfortable and informal situations.

Yeah

Yeah is a relaxed substitute for *yes*. This is a speech pattern among all ethnic groups. Respect calls for *yes*.

Your, Yours

Never say yorn. There is no "n" in *your* or *yours*. This is another word that many children hear, and then grow up with, without correction. Clean it up now. Informal: *Is that mine or yorn?* Formal: *Is that mine or yours?*

You're/Your

Though pronunciation is very similar, these two are spelled differently and have two different meanings. As mentioned earlier, *your* is possessive and *you're* is the contraction for *you are*.

Zoology

Zo. Not zoo. *Zoology* is pronounced *zoh-ology*, not *zoo-ology*. Zo with a long o.

THE ORIGIN OF BLACK ENGLISH

Before judging or categorizing the ways in which people communicate, we must first define terms. What is Black Vernacular English? Does it even exist? Is it a dialect? Idiolect or regional dialect? Is it temporal or is it a part of the public dialect? Should it be condemned or used all the time? Answering these questions with one broad theoretical statement would be impossible, but studying the origin of Black Vernacular English as well as why its prevalence remains in the community, becomes the real issue. Imagine being forced to stop speaking your native tongue, while forced to hear a strange one. What would you do?

Black Vernacular English has an origin that may date back to the year 1619. Africa, the Middle Passage journey, and the Americas may also be suspect in the creation of African American English Dialect. There is a very interesting bond between these factors and their effects on language. At first glance one might doubt that this phenomenon of speech has any ties to the history and culture of the African-American.

Slang and inventive survival dialect in the

African-American community are widely used. BVE is primarily an effect of slavery, since the common languages from the African continent were dissolved by force. As African languages were sifted out of our mental and verbal familiarity, the English language began to work its way into our psyche. Sadly, very few African Americans can speak or read an African language. In actuality, a hybrid of language was being developed without Africans and slave masters even realizing it. New words, innovative expressions, fresh ways of phrasing, and unique spellings began inhabiting the English language from an neo-African or Black point of view. The slave master wasn't realizing that he was allowing Africans to create a new way of speaking here because of the suppression of culture and freedom. Slave masters were confused because they didn't have a plan of attacking communication amongst "slaves" that was highly effective or suppressive. Many slaveholders tried to ban the singing of slaves. Some tried the *bit method*, which consisted of placing a large block or bit in the mouth to prevent communication exchange. Bits, masks, cages, and bridles were also used to prevent disobedience, self suffocation, dirt eating, and the drinking of alcohol. A popular concept was to prohibit slaves from reading and writing but this was an impractical and far-fetched notion on the master's part. To silence anyone (even through force of violence) is nearly impossible. The voice is the gun and the pen is the sword. Captured Africans eventually found ways to acquire knowledge and to communicate.

Once this *language restriction-construction* (LRC) began to take root, Africans embarked upon a new way of hearing and speaking. BVE was born from the cruel institution of slavery, but its devices are still used, embraced, and appreciated by Blacks today because of its effectiveness and creative expression. Language Restriction-Construction is born from a restriction to do one thing devising an ability and free will to create another because of the restriction. The construction of BVE was invented from our limited knowledge of the formal English language. We also must attribute this restriction to Europeans that didn't have a formal pattern of speaking and writing English as well. In the United States, there is no such thing as authentic English. People from England will remind you that west of the Atlantic, English is not spoken. They will say, "You speak *American*, not English."

Many of the patterns in BVE are still used today and they make perfect sense to those familiar with the dialect. The problem arises in the broader world or in our case, the United States of America. Everyone in America does not understand BVE. Some Blacks do not speak and understand BVE. Many European whites do not speak or comprehend BVE. Because the speaking of "so-called" Standard American English is important in this society, it is in the best interest of Blacks desiring entrepreneurial, financial, and social mobility to be able to utilize the language of power and finance. BVE should not be forgotten, forbidden, nor forsaken, but there is a time and a place for all activities, speech patterns, attitudes, behaviors, clothing and lifestyles. Multiple dialects can offer the mobility to work in and out of multicultural environments.

Some of the more common African-American expressions that have shown signs of African origination are the consistent sarcastic teasing remarks used to avoid physical confrontation -- as we know in this country as *playing the dozens*. Many West Africans that I've spoken with have related "the dozens" with a form of verbally teasing friends. Dr. Geneva Smitherman, a speech and African Studies expert, has studied languages from Africa and gives several examples in her book.

African-American speech characteristics that have been fused into the English language are profound and very useful. When speaking Standard American English (SAE), one can lose something in the translation from BVE to SAE. Here's an example. Two ladies are talking about a man who has been unkind to one of the ladies. First the conversation in Black Vernacular English.

Speaker 1: What's up girl? Whatchu gon' do wit 'em?
Speaker 2: Girl, he been trippin from the git.
Speaker 1: 'Scuse me, girlfriend, whatchu gone do?
Speaker 2: Amma drop 'em next week!
Speaker 1: Dats whatchu sed las week.

Now here's the conversation in Mainstream English.

Speaker 1: What's going on friend? What are you going to do with him?
Speaker 2: Girlfriend, he hasn't been acting right since the beginning.
Speaker 1: Excuse me, friend, so what are you going to do?
Speaker 2: I'm going to break up with him next week!
Speaker 1: That's what you told me last week.

The differences between the words, the usage, the accents and the rhythm are clearly identified here. The message is conveyed in BVE and as you should be able to see how meaning can get lost in translation to Standard English. In the neighborhood, I prefer using BVE because it is comfortable, communicable, colorful, rhythmic, and vast. The skill is in the ability to shift gears into the "other English" when needed.

Shifting gears can be called several things. Some would say that it is *selling out* or *assimilation*. Others might call verbal gear shifting a form of adaptation or code switching. It is clear that this skill is what W.E.B. DuBois once alluded to as the *Veil*. The *Veil* is the dual consciousness that inhabits the African-American. He explains this in his book, *The Souls of Black Folk.*

> ...the Negro is a sort of seventh son, born with a veil, and gifted with second-sight in this American world, -- a world which yields him no true self-consciousness, but only lets him see himself through the revelation of the other world. It is a peculiar sensation, this double-consciousness, this sense of always looking at one's self through the eyes of others, of measuring one's soul by the tape of a world that looks on in amused contempt and pity. One ever feels his twoness, -- an American, a Negro; two souls, two thoughts, two unreconciled strivings; two warring ideals in one dark body, whose dogged strength alone keeps it from being torn asunder.

DuBois sums up the African-American experience and its many complexities. The question of dialect switching can be equally complex, but great concern should be taken in knowing both and having the knowledge to use them at the *right* times.

Frederick Douglass also teaches us a lesson in his autobiographical essays and letters. Africans were forbidden to learn how to read and he emphatically points out the Black child's need to learn in this poignant quote from his slave master.

> If you teach that n.... how to read, there would be no keeping him. Learning would *spoil* the best n..... in the world. It would forever unfit him to be a slave. If you give a n.... an inch, he will take an ell (45 inches). A

n..... should know nothing but to obey his master--to do as he is told to do...I now understood what had been to me a most perplexing difficulty--to wit, the white man's power to enslave the black man (literacy).

What makes us so arrogant as to think that learning the language of power and finance isn't important today? The slavemaster's words affirm that the currency of literacy can liberate. It is time for African Americans to embrace literacy more now than ever.

BLACK LEADERS USE STANDARD ENGLISH

The most powerful Black leaders have chosen to speak Standard American English. Even those who claim to promote the constant use of Black English, make it a point to speak as mainstream as possible to embrace mass audiences.

Dr. Martin Luther King, Jr. was classic in his use of language, enunciation, and verbal expression. King's words sounded like music and his metaphors and similes were far better than many of the greatest poets.

The diction of Malcolm X was nearly flawless and Malcolm did this on his own volition (reading various books including dictionaries, psychology, philosophy, and religious works while in prison). Malcolm realized that the best way to impart knowledge was to simply communicate through mainstream American English. Listen to some of Malcolm's recorded speeches. His articulation and precision will make you beam with pride.

And in the creative arena, the delivery of poets, writers, and recording artists have shown to be proving grounds for understanding. Intellectuals like W.E.B. DuBois, James Baldwin, Richard Wright, Dr. Carter G. Woodson, Booker T. Washington, and Ralph Ellison have shown us the social and psychological problems that have plagued the African-American with their exemplary writing. To this day, works from these men still resonate within the African American community.

Even superstar musicians, entertainers, and athletes find it in their best interest to command the language with consistency. Good diction promotes more endorsements, interviews, and exposure. More and more athletes are hiring speech coaches to secure jobs after their athletic careers. It's reassuring to hear athletes discuss their prospective sports because they can discuss the science and philosophy of the competition as well as the amusement of the game. Wouldn't it be embarrassing if NBA players could not speak Standard American English? When someone goes to the microphone or podium to speak, haven't we all felt that nervous tension, because we assume that the speaker will sound illiterate and terrifyingly inarticulate? I don't like that feeling. I'm proud of today's players because most of them have satisfactory speaking abilities. Better speaking skills for athletes can lead to more *playing time* on the microphone during interviews. This, in turn, can lead to endorsements, commercials, analysts positions, and creative content.

We must start realizing that *excellence transcends race*. Speaking Standard American English isn't *selling out* your identity. Using your best diction will enable you to get ahead in the United States. Successful African Americans wouldn't be where they are if the exercised poor communication skills. We as a people have to take the high road that will lead us to the promised land: the land of milk and honey, the road that leads to our success as a people.

There is nothing wrong with a child wanting to be a professional athlete but the odds are too great to take that chance alone (1.1% of Division I NCAA athletes make it into the pros).

Let's teach our children and educate our adults about the pitfalls we all suffer in this war against illiteracy. Study the examples in this book and also see Evelyn B. Dandy's book entitled, *Black Communications: Breaking Down the Barriers*. Two other essential titles are J.L. Dillard's *Black English* and Dr. Geneva Smitherman's *Black Talk [Words and Phrases from the Hood to the Amen Corner]*.

GOOD AND EVIL IN THE LANGUAGE OF HIP HOP

Rap music is Black America's T.V. station.
Chuck D.

In the world of rap music there are many positive and negative points. This chapter will focus on the perils and triumphs of rap's language. I will have to criticize some rap artists intensely because of their destructive nature. Later in the chapter, I will sing praises and give rap its compliments.

Besides many rap artists referring to women in derogatory fashion, there are many other evils in the music's warping of the English language. Intentional misspellings, twisted definitions, and mispronunciation in songs all attribute to a new dialect that is fun to listen to and emulate; but if children are unable to distinguish between the dialect of rap (saturated with Black Vernacular English) and the *great Midwestern dialect,* you will have children that will confuse these same concepts in school, church, home, and with his/her friends. It should be obvious why this can be detrimental.

We must teach children that there is a time and a place for dialects. In Strunk and White's *The Elements of Style,* the writers warn us of language usage that may not be mainstream. In ordinary composition, use orthodox spelling. Do not write *nite* for *night*, *thru* for *through*, *pleez* for *please*, unless you plan to introduce a complete system of simplified spelling and are prepared to take the consequences.

Stick to the rules of English to avoid looking inarticulate and unintelligent. Be on the lookout for other terms used in rap that aren't standard. Expressions and words that are used in rap can be colorful and comfortable in your environment. One should restrict the usage in the situations we've mentioned earlier.

Most rap music is very degrading to Black people. Women take major punishment, morals get thrown out of the window, and the respect for the African American also becomes diminutive. Most rap videos depict young Black men as unemployed, drug dealers, or pimps with a serious appetite for alcohol, narcotics, women, and cars with big rims. Sadly, many non-Blacks think that the majority of Black populations live like this. Where are the rappers with decent clothes, business attire, grammar, and videos that don't exist in "da hood"? Do all Black people live in a war torn ghetto, replete with nefarious activity, and scantily clad women? Do rappers have mothers and sisters they respect enough to pay tribute? What's more, do these rappers ever articulate in a manner that can be understood by most people? They don't have to and aren't obligated, but children need to know that this is a created reality of "life in the hood" video form, because most of these rappers don't live in their portrayed surroundings. Being able to distinguishing the good from the bad is the key. There is a time and place for rap lingo, but it's not in a formal letter to a corporation or on a standardized test in school. Make sure your child is reading and that the child understands the difference between rap's English and Standard American English. If you allow your child to listen to rap, you may want to listen as well.

On the other hand, rap is one of the reasons some children have any self-esteem. It empowers many of our children by saying things that they need to hear. Professional rappers and and basketball players embody the few Black men who make lots of money and who have freedom of speech and power that most Black men will never have. Some rappers choose positive messages warning young people of medical, moral, and emotional dangers, while encouraging knowledge of self, self-love, and the promotion of reading. Just as Jewish content creators would feel obligated to discuss the Holocaust, rap artists should feel obligated to tell stories of triumph, despair, inventions, history, and the *middle passage* realizing "that for 200 hundred years, shipped sailed carrying human cargo." Jazz musician, Donald Byrd, defends rap music by making this statement, "Rap music is a poetic form criticized because many who criticize it cannot do it successfully."

Some rappers have more pugnacious and obscene content, but their lyrics state the truth about the treatment of

Black Americans. Others are considered gentle in lyrical content but manage to instill responsible behavior from treating people with respect to becoming a productive citizen in society. Rap music is a medium that influences heavily on our children and we must monitor (not censor) the lyrics they digest.

Show the distinction between what's right and wrong lyrically. Some rappers exaggerate to reinforce a point. As long as the child realizes that the rap artist is an entertainer, he or she should be able to not take the rapper literally all of the time. This is the responsibility of the parents even though the parents may not get to listen to all of the rap music in the child's collection – although you should.

Rap's strongest allies are the music, beat, bass line, and samples. Many times lyrics aren't understandable because of music drowning out the rapper or the confusion of regional dialect. But most lyrics are easily heard and can be offensive. It is unfortunate, that most rappers are African American buffoons who choose to curse out their audience for a paycheck. We can only hope that better days come so there is more good than evil in rap music.

TEACH MAINSTREAM ENGLISH TO BLACK CHILDREN

In the 21st century, it is imperative that teachers of English spend extra time with their students. There are some school systems that are prolific in their ability to produce high school graduates who cannot read a job application, a simple contract, or a book written for someone 6 grades younger than the 18 year-old "graduate." In the tech age, not only will a person have to be literate in terms of reading a book, but scientific acumen, coding basics, mathematics, and critical thinking skills will place a strain on those who aren't able to decipher more sophisticated manuals, more esoteric instructions, and the incessantly advancing app software. The days of the factory job are just about over and it has been estimated that over 50% of all American citizens will have to create their own job.

It sounds a bit intimidating but literacy is no longer a monolithic concept. It has multiple meanings and must be respected as such. As education becomes more operationalized and beholden to software and the cloud, teachers will have to engage, embrace, and adopt the professional practice of using online pedagogy. A child who can read and operate a mobile phone or tablet will be at least a survivor in the "click" age. With the mastery of the English language along with software app literacy and mastery, we are looking towards serving school populations for the future..

English skills are fundamental. Even though there are Black children diagnosed as LEP (limited-English proficient) and NEP (non-English proficient) steering them in the direction of mainstream English is imperative. Hopefully there aren't any Empiricists and Romantic ideologists teaching in our schools today. Empiricists believed that Africans were brute, savage animals who didn't have the cortical capacity for human language. Empiricists such as John Locke and Carolus Linnaeus believed that Africans had a language similar to primates (chimps and gorillas). Romanticists believed that Africans were simple, unsophisticated children incapable of understanding "esoteric" speech patterns. To avoid such ridiculous stereotypes, we need to know the basics. Choosing not to use mainstream American English is a hindrance for thousands, which was cited in a USA Today article entitled "The Dumbing of the American Mind." The article states the average 17 year old could not successfully understand a bank statement, do relatively simple multiplication and division problems, or spend a concentrated block of time in order to read a book. In Eleanor Wilson Orr's insightful book, *Twice as Less: Does Black English Stand Between Black Students and Success in Math and Science*, she noted that the multitude of students misunderstood prepositions, conjunctions, and relative pronouns which obviously altered the meaning of story problems. But if teachers were sensitive to the nuances and rhythms of Black English as well as the structure of the language (which should have been taught to the teachers in college) there would be more empathy for the capable student. One problem that creeps into the machine is the teacher's lack of responsibility. Many English teachers do not like to "correct" a Black student's diction. This teacher finds himself or herself in a quandary: a place where no self-respecting educator likes to be. Administrators and parents do not help matters by encouraging social promotion (honoring substandard academic progress).

Math, science, and history teachers are correcting their pupils. What makes the English instructor's situation any different? Well, there are unpleasant terms like "correct," "wrong," "right," and "standard" that insult the parents, students, school boards, PTA sponsors, literacy consultants, therapists, and speech pathologists. This is really too bad, because who suffers from the low expectation? This same child who will be penalized during future job interviews, in college, in the business world, at mixed company social gatherings, and for the rest if his or her life. The teacher should not compromise the child's education. Teaching is the role of the teacher; therefore teaching should take place. I've seen full scale arguments develop from this tug-o-war. Parents in some predominantly Black neighborhoods despise teachers who try to correct their child's dialect. I find this ludicrous because the child is in school to learn. Can a person maintain his cultural and linguistic identity if he decides to use Standard English in formal situations like school, social events, and in the workplace? This becomes a most puzzling question because knowledge of self is an internal volition. Problems arise when others attempt to define 'self' by standards concerning what they're comfortable with and tolerant of handling. Arlette Ingram Willis discusses the concept of the 'self' in an article entitled, *Reading the World of School Literacy: Contextualizing the Experience of a Young African American Male*. She allows us to take a peek into her home, where her school aged son is approached with what she calls unintentional cultural insensitivity. Many teachers adopt and exercise this method and cause in many cases irreparable damage. Willis says, "It [the educational system] is built upon a narrow understanding of school knowledge and literacy, which are defined and defended as what one needs to know and how one needs to know it in order to be successful in school and society." She eloquently states this scenario as it relates to her child who is Black, trying to cope with one teacher trying to deliberately obliterate race and ethnicity in the classroom: a virtual impossibility. Though the elimination of Black Vernacular

English in some mainstream situations may be painful, we find that code switching from one dialect to another is useful not only for (receivers) those who don't understand Black English, but for the senders as well. This echoes the writings of Ellison's *Invisible Man*, DuBois' *The Souls of Black Folks*, and Baldwin's *The Fire Next Time*. Willis goes on to discuss the importance of cultural, functional, and critical literacies. Cultural referring to the network of information all competent readers use, functional being the mastery of skills needed to read and write as measured by standardized forms of assessment, and critical literacy which refer to the ideologies that underlie the relationship between power and knowledge in society. Despite these definitions, the new reader needs to master the reading of letters, words, and paragraphs, before anything else.

I have witnessed many deficiencies in speech, writing, and reading. Because we learn language in the first five years in an environment not resembling a school institution, we have no formal training of the English language. As a child, we acquire cues and clues in language. Humans communicate only because they want something, and in the earlier stages of life, we will use what we've been taught or what has worked from experience. If a child can only use fragments to communicate, the teacher would have to provide pedagogy that can help the new speaker and reader to develop sentence construction. We must hold our teachers responsible for their professional duties.

EXPERT COMMENTARY ON BLACK ENGLISH

Cruel people take advantage of those who do not know how to read and write. - Dr. Kingsley Fletcher

Studies consistently demonstrate that educators manifest a generally negative reaction to the "less familiar dialect" in favor of Standard English. Black educators have long recognized the possible socioeconomic disadvantages of speaking a Black dialect in a predominantly White society. *There is empirically based evidence of teacher bias against Black students.* [These children] with this pattern are candidates for coded categories such as "slow learner," "learning disabled," "intellectually impaired" or "not a strong potential candidate." Black English speakers are presented with more obstacles to success than are speakers of Standard English. - Betsy Winsboro and Irvin Soloman

Although use of language may not matter in menial jobs, it does matter for the better paying jobs (and for entrance into the professional schools), where employers seek reasons to reject Blacks. - Darwin Turner

Research on the effect of language on employability indicates that in fact the better jobs do go to the speakers of Standard English. - Judy Floyd Robbins

Standard English is the common language, the one we use when we want to speak across cultural barriers. And like the workers on the Biblical Tower of Babel, we will be unable to accomplish anything unless we understand one another. Each English has its time and place. - Daniel Heller

The neighborhood language becomes what the West Africans call the sweet language. That then makes a person bilingual. He or she speaks Standard English, which is needed in the marketplace. He or she also speaks the sweet language, which is used to make contact with a beloved, a family member, a friend. I think what should be taught is the Standard English language. The other languages of the neighborhood are so in flux that you really can't teach them. They can learn, but you can't teach them. - Maya Angelou

The school has seemed unable to recognize and take up the potentially positive interactive verbal interpretive habits learned by Black American children, rural and urban, within their families and on the streets. [Black students] have skills that would benefit all youngsters: keen listening and observational skills, quick recognition of roles, rapid-fire dialogue, hard-driving argumentation, succinct recapitulation of an event, striking metaphors, and comparative analyses based on unexpected analogies. - John Baugh

Part of the problem could be that individuals look down on people they consider socially inferior. - Weaver and Eller

Teachers' and administrators' perceptions of students can be a factor in the school's own culture and climate: —The more open the climate of the school, the less alienated students tend to be. - Wayne Hoy

There may be conflicting views about empirical determinants, but African American students tend to be outcasts in American schools - the group which widespread notions of academic inferiority prevail. - K. Ainsworth-Darnell

A teacher's bias against a student's Black English dialect may trigger lower teacher expectations and lower student performance. - Susan Masland

According to Oates, anti-Black bias among White teachers is more prevalent than the same bias from Black teachers. White teachers' perceptions are significantly more consequential to the performance of African American students. - R.F. Ferguson

Although all languages should be accepted and considered equal, the reality is that Standard American English is what is expected by society. - Lynn Isenbarger

A whole language approach to language arts instruction is beneficial to Black children and that it can be compatible with Afrocentric teaching models. - E.B. Dandy

References

Aaron, R., & Powell, G. (1982). Feedback Practices as a Function of Teacher and Pupil Race During Reading Group Instruction. *The Journal of Negro Education, 51*(1), 50. doi:10.2307/2294649

Baldwin, J., Schapiro, S., Lewis, J., & Karefa-Smart, G. (2017). *The fire next time.* Köln, Germany: Taschen.

Ball, A., & Lardner, T. (1997, 12). Dispositions toward Language: Teacher Constructs of Knowledge and the Ann Arbor Black English Case. *College Composition and Communication, 48*(4), 469. doi:10.2307/358453

Beck, S. W., & Olah, L. N. (2001). *Perspectives on language and literacy: Beyond the here and now.* Cambridge, MA: Harvard Educational Review.

Blake, R., & Cutler, C. (2003, 06). AAE and Variation in Teachers' Attitudes: A Question of School Philosophy? *Linguistics and Education, 14*(2), 163-194. doi:10.1016/s0898-5898(03)00034-2

Blase, J., & Blase, J. (1999, 08). Principals' Instructional Leadership and Teacher Development: Teachers' Perspectives. *Educational Administration Quarterly, 35*(3), 349-378. doi:10.1177/00131619921968590

Boykin, A. W., Tyler, K. M., & Miller, O. (2005, 09). In Search of Cultural Themes and Their Expressions in the Dynamics of Classroom Life. *Urban Education, 40*(5), 521-549. doi:10.1177/0042085905278179

Cicetti-Turro, D. (2007, 04). Straight Talk: Talking Across Race in Schools. *Multicultural Perspectives, 9*(1), 45-49. doi:10.1080/15210960701334102

Craig, H. K., & Washington, J. A. (2002, 02). Oral Language Expectations for African American Preschoolers and Kindergartners. *American Journal of Speech-Language Pathology, 11*(1), 59. doi:10.1044/1058-0360(2002/007)

Dandy, E. B. (1991). *Black communications: Breaking down the barriers* Chicago,IL.African American Images.

Delpit, L. D. (2006). *Other people's children: Cultural conflict in the classroom.* New York: New Press.

Delpit, L. D., & Dowdy, J. K. (2008). *The skin that we speak: Thoughts on language and culture in the classroom.* New York: New Press.

Diangelo, R., & Sensoy, Ö. (2010, 05). "OK, I Get It! Now Tell Me How to Do It!": Why We Can't Just Tell You How to Do Critical Multicultural Education. *Multicultural Perspectives, 12*(2), 97-102. doi:10.1080/15210960.2010.481199

Downey, D. B., & Pribesh, S. (2004, 10). When Race Matters: Teachers' Evaluations of Students' Classroom Behavior. *Sociology of Education, 77*(4), 267-282. doi:10.1177/003804070407700401

DuBois, W.E.B., (1903). The Souls of Black Folk. Dover Press.

Eglantine, C. C. (2011). *Self-Affirmation: Claude Steele.* Mauritius: TypPRESS.

Elhoweris, H., Mutua, K., Alsheikh, N., & Holloway, P. (2005, 01). Effect of Children's Ethnicity on Teachers' Referral and Recommendation Decisions in Gifted and Talented Programs. *Remedial and Special Education, 26*(1), 25-31. doi:10.1177/07419325050260010401

Ferguson, R. F. (2003, 07). Teachers' Perceptions and Expectations and the Black-White Test Score Gap. *Urban Education, 38*(4), 460-507. doi:10.1177/0042085903038004006

Ferguson, R. F. (2003, 07). Teachers' Perceptions and Expectations and the Black-White Test Score Gap. *Urban Education, 38*(4), 460-507. doi:10.1177/0042085903038004006

Gershenson, S., Holt, S., & Papageorge, N. (n.d.). Who Believes in Me? The Effect of Student-Teacher Demographic Match on Teacher Expectations. *SSRN Electronic Journal.* doi:10.2139/ssrn.2633993

Glaser, C. B., & Smalley, B. S. (1995). *More power to you!: How women can communicate their way to success.* New York, NY: Warner Books.

Herrnstein, R.J., & Murray, C. (1997). *The bell curve: Intelligence and class structure in American life.* New York: Simon&Schuster.

Hoy, W. K. (1990). Organizational Climate and Culture: A Conceptual Analysis of the School Workplace. *Journal of Educational and Psychological Consultation, 1* (2), 149-16 P8. doi:10.1207/s1532768xjepc0102_4

Isenbarger, L., & Zembylas, M. (2006, 01). The emotional labour of caring in teaching. *Teaching and Teacher Education, 22*(1), 120-134. doi:10.1016/j.tate.2005.07.002

Jencks, C., & Phillips, M. (1998). The Black-White Test Scope Gap: Why It Persists and What Can Be Done. *The Brookings Review, 16*(2), 24. doi:10.2307/20080778

Masland, S. W. (1979, 03). Black Dialect and Learning to Read: What is the Problem? *Journal of Teacher Education, 30*(2), 41-44. doi:10.1177/002248717903000211

McWhorter, J. H. (2001). *Losing the race self-sabotage in Black America.* New York: Free Press.

Orr, E. W. (1987). *Twice as less: Black English and the performance of black students in mathematics and science.* New York: Norton.

Perry, T. E., & Delpit, L. E. (1998). *The Real Ebonics Debate: Power, Language, and the Education of African-American Children.* Beacon Press.

Reeves, Richard (2017). Race gaps in SAT math scores are big as ever. Brookings Institute.

Steele, C., Aronson, J., & Spencer, S. (n.d.). Stereotype Threat. *Encyclopedia of Social Psychology.* doi:10.4135/9781412956253.n558

Strunk, W., & White, E. B. (2016). *The elements of style.* North Charleston, SC: CreateSpace Independent Publishing Platform.

Thernstrom, A. M., & Thernstrom, S. (2003). *No excuses: Closing the racial gap in learning.* New York: Simon & Schuster.

Wells, H. G. (2017). *Invisible man.* Place of publication not identified: Vintage Classics.

Willis, A. I. (1995, 04). Reading the World of School Literacy: Contextualizing the Experience of a Young African American Male. *Harvard Educational Review, 65*(1), 30-50. doi:10.17763/haer.65.1.22226055362w11p5

Garrard McClendon, Ph.D. is an associate professor at Chicago State University. His research areas are in student perceptions and expectations, school finance, and school law. He has held teaching positions at the Culver Academies, Purdue University, Calumet College of St. Joseph's, Bishop Chatard and Bishop Noll Institute. He holds degrees from Wabash College, Valparaiso University, and Loyola University.

McClendon is the Executive Director of the Milton and Ruby McClendon Education Foundation, and holds board positions for the Sheilah A. Doyle Foundation and Donda's House Foundation. McClendon has won an Emmy Award, One Region Award, Associated Press Award, IBA Cardinal Award, a Monarch Award, and NAACP Champion Award.

He is the author of Donda's Rules, Ebonics Empathy, Ebonics Anthology, 99 Problems But Barack Wasn't One, and The Excuses of Black Folk.

Duthga Press

www.ingramcontent.com/pod-product-compliance
Lightning Source LLC
Chambersburg PA
CBHW021132300426
44113CB00006B/402